Voice of Our Ancestors

By Wulf Sorenson
(thought to be Heinrich Himmler)

with introduction by David Lane

Introduction

For several years I have been writing about the methods that certain aware or initiated individuals of the past have used to keep old wisdom alive and identify tyrants without being burned at the stake, tortured by the inquisition, forced to recant and so on.

One method among many was to disguise messages in the myths and religions and in folkish tales. Wise men look first to the numbers for a wisdom of the ancients. While the words of men are subject to interpretation, change, slanting or translation, the relationship of number is forever constant. Thus, the greatest truths are concealed in number and we read, "But Snow White, over the seven mountains with the seven dwarves is a thousand timed fairer than you."

In this manner messages are identified and interpretation of the parables and allegories is aided. Such devices are often called "Hermetic" (hidden) and may conceal up to seven distinct and separate messages. Wulf Sorensen has given a masterful interpretation of the Snow White fairy tale in "Voice Of Our Ancestors". We hope you will enjoy and that the message will aid you and others in the search for what has been destroyed by tyrants of church and state during two thousand years of dark ages of religion and of governmental suppression.

David Lane

Voice of Our Ancestors

There they hang on the wall, one hundred ninety-six little plaques in oval, gilded frames. And there are still far fewer than there ought to have been. All the frames in the upper rows show only a name with a couple of dates on white paper.

But in the lower rows they become alive. The portraits begin about the time of the Thirty Years War. They are fine miniatures, carefully painted with a pointed brush on ivory, which has long since yellowed.

One cannot but think of the difficulty the artist must have had in capturing those stern, proud features with his soft, marten-hair brush. All of the white ruffled collars, the lace, the puffed sleeves and on the "gentlemen, " the jabots have a frivolous effect on these portraits dating from the beginning of the eighteenth century. "Ladies"? "Gentlemen"? No, indeed! In spite of the velvet and silk there is not a "lady" nor a "gentleman" among them. They are all women and men - and that says far more than the "gentleman" of today.

For they. there on the wall, living again in their portraits - were free! This is what we have come to, that we must banish our ancestors to pictures or vital statistics on the wall in order to give them a faint presence in our dim memories. Ancestors? People today do not even know the birth dates and death dates of their own parents. Of course, they are written down somewhere. It is a wonder if one knows even a little about his grandfather, not to mention his great-grandfather.

As for great-great-grandfather, one does not think about him at all. as if he had never existed. Earlier - much earlier - things were different. That was before words had become but mere merchandise, used to concoct lies, when a man still lived by his word; then it was not necessary to write down and record one's ancestors. That was a time when the living flow of blood from son to father, from father to grandfather and great-grandfather and great-great-grandfather still had not been choked off. It had not yet sunk, as it has today, so deep beneath all of the alien values within mind and soul, that most of us can no longer hear its rustle, even in the stillest hour. Once the whole past dwelt in the hearts of the living. And from this past the present and the future grew upward like the strong limbs of a healthy tree. And today? They laugh at the fables of our Folk, They do not even understand them. Nevertheless, that which remains with us from the "Once upon a time" of our fables, serves as a reminder, a finger showing us the way back into the millennia of our great past.

You believe that we have no use for what is past and gone? Nonsense! The man in whose breast the "Once upon a time" of his race is no longer awake - has no future which truly belongs to him. How timely would be the appearance of a man who would teach us again the meaning of our fables, and show us that our struggle for the freedom of the earth which has borne us was, also, the struggle of our ancestors a hundred and a thousand years ago!

Did you know that when you read about Snow White and the Wicked Queen who came over the mountains, that those mountains she had to cross each time she came to kill Snow White were the Alps, and that the Queen came from Rome, the deadly enemy of everything Nordic? Think about the Queen's Daily query: "Mirror, mirror on the wall, Who is the fairest of them all? " When you think of this saying think about Rome, which could not rest until everything Nordic, bright and joyful was exterminated, and only darkness remained - dark like the Wicked queen in the fairy tale, so that she could be the fairest in all the land, after everything white was dead.

That which came over the southern

mountains to us tolerated no peers. Everything had to kneel before it and kiss its feet. When the queen came over the Alps the first time, dressed as a peddler from a

distant land, she offered Snow White a bewitched corset - bewitched because it was alien. Then she pulled the laces so tight that Snow White fainted and fell. The emissaries of Rome bound the Nordic spirit in the suffocating bonds of alien concepts and deceitful words.

But the queen's ruinous plan did not succeed, The dwarves - the good spirits of the Folk - came and freed Snow White.

The Frisians crushed the Roman emissaries who tried to break the strength of our people with their doctrines of misery and servitude, For nearly a thousand years the Nordic tribes struggled against the poison from Sinai, which gradually fouled their blood.

And when the vain queen again asked her mirror, the answer was: "... but Snow White, over the seven mountains with the seven dwarves is a thousand times fairer than you. " Driven by her restless jealousy, the queen came over the snowy wall of the Alps with a new deception. She offered Snow White a magnificent glittering Comb, the most exotic thing she had ever seen. The "Holy Roman Empire" diverted the Nordic will-of-action away from its natural course; one after another, Nordic leaders have gone off to Rome and the consequence has been turmoil and Roman law in our land, which has enchained our Nordic pride. It began with Karl, the eternally cursed Frank, murderer of Saxons. From Aller to Verdun, the blood of the most noble or our people is on his hands. In recognition for his deeds, the Roman priests bestowed upon Karl the title of "The Great. "

Silent forever are the lips of our Folk who named this wretched Frank, "Karl the Saxon slayer"!

Despite this, the Nordic spirit remained unbroken; the Wicked queen still was not the fairest in the land. And so, for a third visit she came and presented Snow White with a rosy-cheeked, but poisoned apple. The first bite stuck in Snow White's throat and caused her to faint as if dead. This apple symbolized the rejection of our

own nature, the abandonment Of tribal ways.

"As if dead, " the fairy tale says, acknowledges the enormous strength which slumbers in our people, recognizing that one day will come the great hour, when that strength will mightily throw off the chains of Sinai. Has it yet come, this long awaited hour?

"Snow White" is but one of the hundreds and hundreds of age-old Nordic tales which remind us, with as many different images, of the difficulties, the oppression and the deep wisdom of our ancestors.

And as Rome cracked its whip over our land, mercilessly annihilating every genuine manifestation of our own nature, our wise forebears wove into these tales, using colorful symbols and allegory, a legacy of our heritage. But Rome's influence extended over our tales and sagas, falsifying them, giving them new meaning and made advantageous to Roman domination. Thus, it was that our people no longer could understand the voice of our ancestors, that we went astray these many centuries. becoming more and more alienated from our own ways and enslaved to Rome, and thus to Judah. Only he who bears his own soul, living and burning in his breast, Is an individual - a master.

And he who abandons his own kind is a slave. The key to freedom lies within us! Now we must hearken again to the voice of our ancestors and protect our essence from alien influences, protect that which wants to grow out of our own souls. Stronger than any army is the man who wields the power which resides within him!

Reflectively, i look over the long rows of my ancestors. The last members reach so far back that hardly more than a name and a date on a sheet of paper remain. Yet their voices come alive in my blood, because their blood is my blood.

I think of how the French-speaking monks came from Switzerland to convert our forefathers, the Goths and the Vandals. Even their deadly enemies, the Romans said: "Where the Goths are, there virtue rules. And where the Vandals are, there even the Romans become chaste. "

And to such men the commandments

from Sinai were offered as guiding lights for their lives! Can one understand why these men laughed when they heard those commandments, which demanded that they not commit acts they never would have dreamed of committing?

Can one understand that they raised their swords in wrath when the monks told them that they were "born in sin" - these best of the Goths, whose very name means "The Good Ones"?

Cannot one understand the unspeakable contempt with which these noble men regarded those who promised them a reward in heaven for abstaining from doing things which, according to their own nature, were beneath the dignity even of animals?

To such men the commandments

were brought; men infinitely superior in human dignity and morality than the monks who brought them. For countless generations they had lived far above the moral plateau on which the commandments from Sinai then operated. Thousands of years before the time of the "Christ" the monks claimed to represent, our ancestors had sown the seeds of culture and civilization throughout the world on their fruitful voyages and wanderings.

When I contemplate the small portraits and see in their firmly composed faces the expressions of my ancestors, which compel no more notice of these times, it seems as if we have descended from a high, high ladder - a ladder which we must yet again climb. Nowadays, it is seldom that we can even appear to be like

they were. They were on intimate terms with Allfather and did not need to call on halo-wearing intermediaries when they wished to speak to him. And even then, they did not know how to beg; they were too strong, too proud and too healthy for supplication.

Blessings prayed for are not true blessings! They wanted nothing of gifts; either they already had everything they wanted or, if they lacked something, they got it for themselves. Their creed was a saying as brief as a wink and as clear and deep as a mountain stream: "DO RIGHT AND FEAR NO ONE! "

As for their religion, there was no necessity to put it into words, which suited a people who were naturally frugal with their words anyway. They carried their spiritual consciousness deep within their souls; it served them like a compass needle which always steers a ship on its proper course.

Was that not a better religion than one which must be written down in a thick book, lest it be forgotten - and which one cannot properly understand until a priest comes and interprets what is written there? And even then, an act of faith is required to believe that this intricate interpretation is correct.

In their day, faith grew from the blood and it was knowledge. Today it must be learned, for it is an alien faith, unable to strike roots in our blood. It is dogma and doctrine which none can know and which most of us silently renounce, because it is contrary to nature and reason. Tell me - have we become better since taking on this new religion? A great wordless sorrow resides in the breast of most of us, a boundless sense of homelessness, because the way of our ancestors lives on eternally in our Nordic blood like a dream.

We want, once again, to be free of sin - like our ancestors were. We are tired of being humble and small and weak and all the other things demanded of us by a god who despises his own creations and looks on the world as a den of corruption. We

Robert Jay Mathews – one of those who stand till last end…. Eternal gratitude to hero of our race.

want to be proud again, and great and strong, and to do things for ourselves!

How different are those faces there on the wall from the faces of today! Only if one looks very closely does one still find a trace of that clarity of the features in the present generation.

What lived so dominantly in our ancestors that it showed in their faces has disappeared back into our blood to dream. That is why faces so often deceive us today. Many a person whose hair color and eye color come from the south, still have the greatest part of their blood from Nordic fathers. And many who appear forgotten by the last two thousand years bear their bright hair and grey or blue eyes only as a deceptive mask, for their blood bears no trace of their fathers from the Northland. The one has only the appearance of the alien and retains his Nordic blood. The other has taken the blood of the alien and retains his Nordic face as an illusory mask. Which is better?

Today, one must look into a person's eyes and see whether or not they are still firm, shining and keen.

The soul is illuminated through the eyes and it does not deceive. There were many a rebel among those there on the wall, and men who left home; many had refused to bend to those with power. They could not go crooked, these fellows. They preferred poverty abroad over submission at home. But they did not stay poor for long. Those who went abroad followed the restless stream of their blood, which gave them no rest until they had found themselves; rejecting that which was foreign to them and flowing into the bloodstream of their fathers, and so became conscious links in the chain of ancestors, closing the great kindred circle.

When one of these came home again - and they all came home - he had become a calm, complete man. It is hard to describe this quality of completeness. If others are babbling in confusion, and such a man utters softly only a couple of words, then all the others will understand and become quiet and attentive. And such a man does not ask questions; others ask him! Look at their eyes; just as they mastered life, so they stood on intimate terms with death.

To them death was life's trusted companion. Those same eyes show up among them even in the most recent generations. There is one of them; Erik was his name and he fell at Kemmel. The steel helmet on his head seems to be a part of him. His mouth is a hard, straight line. But in his twenty-year-old eyes twinkles a silent laugh. And with this laugh, foreign to his mouth, and a wink, saluting with his fist against his breast, beckoning as he steps past, Erik greeted death. I cannot imagine this Erik, with bent knee and plaintive voice, begging some god up in the clouds for mercy and help.

This is the way I picture him: leaping up from a crouch and with a fierce shout, plunging his great sword into a charging enemy - then, still in the same leap, being struck by an arrow and collapsing back to the ground with his final thought, " I gave my best for Germany! "

Erik seized the bitter cup with a proud laugh and drank it down in a single draught without a grimace. And he likely rapped the cup with a fingernail, so that all could hear it was empty.

He did not pray, "Father, let this cup pass from me. " He reached out and seized it for it himself, for he knew... everything necessary is good! Beneath Erik's portrait is his motto, written in his own firm, clear hand: "Let a man be noble, benevolent, loyal and good. " Does that not say far more than those commandments Moses

David Eden Lane

had issued to the depraved rabble in the desert, in order to make that horde grasp the rudiments of humanity?

The Commandments were appropriate for that Hebraic bunch. Even the Egyptians had driven them out of their lands. Even as slaves the Hebrews Were too wicked and infected Egyptian life. The Hebrews - the chosen people of god! It is ludicrous that anyone take it seriously. A commandment presupposes a transgression. One can recognize from the mere necessity for such commandments (which demand nothing more than the barest behavior required to claim the designation "human beings") to what kind of creatures they had been given creatures truly entitled to claim no more than a resemblance to human beings.

To the men of the North these

commandments were a slander, an unforgivable insult to their sacred blood.

So, there rose out of the burning indignation of the Nordic blood a Wittekind[1], who returned again and again to lead his people into battle against the doctrines from Sinai. For these teachings are a deadly poison to our blood. You ask - when will Wittekind return no more? Hearken: Wittekind will die only with the last Northman!

Seventy million Aryans on this glorious earth are more than enough for anything that comes from Sinai. The last remnant who are still pure will still be

---

[1] [Wittekind was Saxon Chief who lead resistance against Charlemagne, King of the Holy Roman Empire, who forced Christianity on the German people. Wittekind was symbolic of Northern Paganism and all out resistance against domination.] So long as a single Aryan lives, Wittekind is alive and the world is not safe from him!

poised when swords resound on shields and the bugles sound for the last, great battle of this wretched millennium.

He who slumbers still, whose blood is dull and sour, no glory for him! He will be thoughtlessly trampled underfoot by the valiant who rush into battle down every street of Aryan homelands.

An ancient custom among our kind has remained alive even to the present day in most parts of our Northland. There was a time when it seemed that this practice, handed down to us from our forefathers, would die out. But it has been revived - and the time is at hand when all our great and beautiful people will again recognize the significance of this custom and be made sound by it.

Our ancestors gave to each child a

powerful name, full of joy and vital energy. Actually, they only lent him this name. And it became a shining hope for the child, far ahead of him on his life's course.

The child bore this name in his soul like his most precious treasure, for it was to him both a goal and a sacred responsibility.

This name strengthened the child's soul as he developed into a conscious, mature individual.

When the child had become a youth, the elders of the kindred gathered for a celebration, at which they decided whether or not the developed character of the young man suited the name which had been given to him. If the man and the name were found to be in harmony, then his name was given to him for life. Otherwise, the young man chose a suitable name for himself one which characterized his nature. So it came to be that our ancestors were like their names and their names like them. And so their name carried weight like a rune-carved sword, like their word and a handshake, like yea and nay.

In Christian times our ancestors were compelled by the new law from abroad to adopt still another name; it was written down in the church register, primarily for the benefit of the census taker. The authorities were obliged to write the living heathen name of a man beside his characterless Christian name in his register, lest it become nothing but a list of phantoms.

In those times the most upright men

and the proudest women sprung forth from our race.

I step closer to the rows of pictures and read the names. The oldest are: Helge, Fromund, Meinrad, Markward, Ran, Waltari, Eigel, Asmus, Bjoern. Peculiar names, are they not? They are names born from the great language of our people. There is nothing foreign in them, no spurious sound. They ring true to the ear. These names taste of the salty sea, of the heavy, fruitful earth, of air and sunshine - and of the homeland. Do you notice that?

A few will notice - but all too few. Their own language has become foreign to them and has nothing more to say to them. After these first rows our ancestors began to name their sons Gottlieb, Christian, Farchgott, Leberecht, Christoph (which mean: God-lover, Christ- worshipper.

God-fearer, Righteous-liver, Christ-carrier)... Still later came the names Paulus, Johannes, Petrus, Christophorus, Korbinianus, Stephanus, Karolus. By those times our forefathers had no other names. Do you feel how something has been broken in these men, how they have become alienated from their own nature? Do you feel how steeply the ladder descends?

A destiny is locked up in the transformation of these names. It is not the destiny of an individual or of a clan, but of a whole people - our Folk. But then something strange happened. Those who had been named Karolus and Paulus by their fathers suddenly regarded these names as annoying, alien, unsuitable, ridiculous. And now comes the generation that went into the Great War. The names with little iron crosses behind the dates on which they fell - a mere 20 or even fewer years from their birth dates, read: Jochen, Dieter, Asmus, Erwin, Walter. Roland, Georg... These are the names we still have today.

And what are the names of our youngest, those who carry their names into the third millennium after the time of Nordic self-forgiveness? Gerhardt, Hartmut, Deitrich, Ingo, Dagwin, Guenther, Hellmut, Gernot, Dagmar, Ingeborg, Helga... Has the Great War done this? The names tell the story.

A few men wear priestly garments. But the painter has given us a clue. And whoever is able to find this clue can see how little or how much the strong heart of the man is darkened by the shadow of the black robes he wears.

The paintings are all bust portraits, nevertheless in one of them the artist shows a hand. It is a strong, sinewy hand, of the sort which could steer a ship through a storm.

The black book in his hand looks like a frivolous toy. Such a hand does not bless an enemy; it crushes him. His name is Frith. That is a strange name for a priest. "Frith" means -peace robber. " Another portrait shows a man with grey, windswept hair. He has a hawkish nose and in his eyes one perceives unlimited vision. Did Ran really bow his head in remorse, repentance and humility? Did he really despise the world and place his confidence in a power other than his own?

I know why fate ordained that these men must wear the black robes; had it not been for them, there would be far fewer heathens in the North today; without them there would be many more who would have exchanged their own image of God for an alien one and would have grown weary of their own strength and the world; and many more would have been seduced by the alien doctrine into becoming its slaves and forgetting their own blood.

They are true saints, for they have preserved their healthy inner selves. despite the priests cassocks. They fought the enemy with his own weapon. People called them "HEATHENS". A few were so proud of this title that they incorporated it into their names, as one might don a precious jewel. For the heathen is one who remains true to himself and his kind, whose blood flows pure in his veins. And this pure blood regards the world with neither the hateful sneer of Sinai or the

weak knees of Nazareth. It bears divinity, pure, clear and beautiful in its red stream, so long as the race endures. None of these men has ever sought God. One does not seek that which dwells in one's own soul.

None of these men has ever been torn with doubt about the divine. Only he who betrays the divinity in himself and offers his soul to an alien god knows such doubt. Doubt is eternal where there is the eternal alien, and thereby the eternal unknown.

The Christian is an eternal doubter.

Can any man be loyal, who is disloyal to himself? Can any man be great, who is consumed with a longing to return to dust? Can any man be strong, who loves weakness? Can any man be proud, who wanders along in humility? Can any man be pure, who regards himself born in sin? Can any man be happy in this world, who despises the world? And can any man bear the Creator in his soul, who despises divine Creation?

What a strange god you Christians have, who created you upright, but who commands you to crawl to him on your knees!

We heathens do not beg to our Creator; it would be an insult to the divinity in our souls.

Nor do we heathens come to the Creator to complain. We do not proclaim our failures to the world and least of all not to the Creator. We seek to overcome our faults and to grow.

Our way is not complaining, but anger - and first of all anger against ourselves. Nor do we repent, we heathens, because we cannot be cowardly; we have the courage to stand by our deeds. Why have you Christians made the name "Heathen" an insult? You should not peddle your pettiness in the streets, for it permits people to see that the love you are commanded to display is bound up with hate, and that the forgiveness your religion requires of you is burdened with your desire for vengeance. Only the envious stoop to insults.

We see your envy and are ashamed for you, since many of you are still brothers of our blood.

There was a time when it was a disgrace to be a Christian. But then you began to conquer the masses and so you were able to turn the tables and make virtue a disgrace. Then you labeled us the "strange" ones and called us heathens. We have remained "strange", despite your insults. We will never be a mass or a herd. Do you know that there are, also, many among you who are "strange" as we are?

Why do you not throw away the beggar's rags which cover the noble garments of your manhood?

Are you ashamed to be "strange"? Afraid to be called heathens? When you Christians have finished burying your god in the sky - come to us; we heathens will again show you the Creator. And do not think we have settled accounts with you Christians. We weigh silently - but we do not weigh with false weights.

We do not deceive the God in us, since we do not deceive ourselves. And as we have weighed justly, so have we calculated, so we would be reckoned with justly by God for our souls You see, we do not repent, since we have nothing to repent. Our value lacks nothing. We retained and preserved our whole worth And now you weigh! And when you have weighed. calculated and evaluated, ask your envious spirit how much you have lost. He who has lost nothing of his worth is without envy - and without hatred for us heathens.

The petty man hates whatever is superior to him, while the great man admires it. The petty man pities whatever is beneath him, while the great man scorns it, if it merits his scorn, or he helps it up. There in his cradle lies my son, reaching, reaching gleefully toward his ancestors' portraits on the wall.

This tiny, laughing bundle of life is the next step of the future of my race. I was the last step. He is the next. And behind me I see the path of my race passing back through the distant millennia until it is dimmed by the mist of time - for the generations which came before the earliest on the wall are, also, real. My race's entire path through time i do not know - but, i do know that i live and that i am only a link in the chain in which no link must fail, so long as my people live.

Otherwise, I never would have been. For generations a parchment-bound book has been passed down through our family i open it and inscribe a yellowed page for my son: "Your life is not of this day and not of tomorrow. It is of the thousand years which came before you and the thousand years to come after you. During the thousand years before you, your blood was purely preserved, so that you would be who you are. Now you must preserve your blood, so that all of the generations of the next thousand years will honor you and thank you. "

That is the meaning of life, that divinity, awakens in the blood. But only in pure blood does it live!

Of whom have I spoken? Of my ancestors? They are only a symbol of the Folk of which i am a living part.

To whom have I spoken? To my son? My son is only a part of my Folk. The wisdom of a thousand generations slumbers in you. Waken it and you have found the key which will open the doors of your truest aspirations. Only he who esteems himself is worthy of being a man.

Only he is a man who bears the living past and future in himself, for only he is able to stand above the present hour. And only he who is master of the present is successful; he alone is fulfilled. As only in fulfillment is divinity. Thus sayeth the Voice of our Ancestors...

The Pagan Snow White And The Evil Queen Christianity.

WULF SORENSEN

(thought to be Heinrich Himmler)

Abb. 170 Kurt Schmid-Ehmen, Hoheitsadler, Luitpoldarena, Nürnberg

CPSIA information can be obtained
at www.ICGtesting.com
Printed in the USA
BVHW011914250922
647952BV00002B/31

9 781682 042939